TI-92 and *The Geometer's Sketchpad* Masters

Glencoe

Geometry
Concepts and Applications

**Glencoe
McGraw-Hill**

New York, New York   Columbus, Ohio   Woodland Hills, California   Peoria, Illinois

The Geometer's Sketchpad® is a registered trademark of
Key Curriculum Press, 1150 65th Street, Emeryville, California, 94608.

Glencoe/McGraw-Hill

*A Division of The **McGraw·Hill** Companies*

Send all inquiries to:
Glencoe/McGraw-Hill
8787 Orion Place
Columbus, OH 43240

Geometry
TI-92 and The Geometer's Sketchpad Masters

ISBN: 0-02-834827-3

4 5 6 7 8 9 10   024   08 07 06 05 04

CONTENTS

CONTENTS

How to Use
The *TI-92 and Geometer's Sketchpad Masters*

The activities in this booklet, like the Graphing Calculator Exploration activities in the text, introduce students to the exciting possibilities of dynamic geometry. Using technology, students can draw and measure geometric figures with great accuracy and then transform the figures by dragging to observe which geometric relationships change or stay the same. Results of calculations and measurements are updated automatically as the student drags points or other parts of a figure in a construction. Parts of figures can be hidden or displayed to show features that are most important in a given situation.

This booklet includes:

• activities using *The Geometer's Sketchpad* that parallel the Graphing Calculator Explorations in the Student Edition,

• one additional technology activity per chapter that uses the TI-92 graphing calculator,

• instructions for *The Geometer's Sketchpad* that parallel the additional TI-92 activity.

You will probably want to allot some time at the beginning of the course for individual or group instruction in the use of the graphing calculator and software. Later, students can refer to the manual for *The Geometer's Sketchpad* and the TI-92 Guidebook. These books contain a wealth of good information. They also discuss other special features of the technology.

For questions about the TI-92 graphing calculator, students can also refer to the TI-92 Quick Reference Guide on page 1 of the Student Edition and the TI-92 Tutorial on pages 758-761 of the Student Edition.

Nested Figures

The Geometer's Sketchpad lets you draw many attractive geometric figures that display interesting patterns. The following steps can be used for one such figure.

Step 1 Select the Segment tool from the Toolbox on the left side of the screen. Draw a 4-sided figure like the first figure below.

Step 2 Choose the Selection Arrow tool from the Toolbox. Hold down the Shift key and click on each side of the figure you drew. The second figure shows what you should see on the screen once you have done this.

Step 3 Move the cursor to the menu bar at the top of the screen. Place the cursor on Construct. Press and hold the mouse button down. Move down the Construct menu to highlight Point at Midpoint. Then release the mouse button. You will see four new points, as in the third figure. The points are highlighted, indicating that they are selected.

Step 4 Go back to the Construct menu and choose Segment. When you release the mouse button, you have a 4-sided figure inside the original figure, as shown in the last figure.

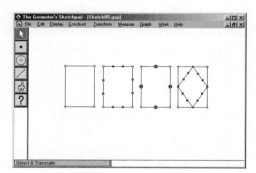

Try These

1. If they are not still selected, select all the sides of the smaller 4-sided figure from Step 4. Then repeat Steps 3 and 4. Describe the results.

2. Go through 3 more rounds with Steps 3 and 4. Describe the figure on the screen after you have done this. (If you have access to a printer, you may want to print out the figure.)

1-6

TI-92 Graphing Calculator

Area of Parallelograms

Use a TI-92 graphing calculator and the following steps to draw a parallelogram and find its area.

Step 1   Use 5:Segment on the F2 menu to draw a segment that is neither horizontal nor vertical.

Step 2   Use 7:Vector on the F2 menu to draw a horizontal arrow at the bottom of the screen. (In mathematics, arrows like this are called *vectors.*)

Step 3   Select 1:Translation from the F5 menu. Move the cursor to the middle of the segment. When you see "TRANSLATE THIS SEGMENT," press ENTER. Then move the cursor to the vector. When the calculator displays "BY THIS VECTOR," press ENTER.

Step 4   On the F3 menu, select 4:Polygon. Move the cursor to the bottom point of the segment. When you see "THIS POINT," press ENTER. Move the cursor to the bottom point of the second segment. When you see "THIS POINT," press ENTER again. Go to the top point of the second segment, then the top point of the first segment, and finally back to the bottom point of the first segment, pressing ENTER for each point. You now have a parallelogram.

Step 5   To find the area of the parallelogram, select 2:Area on the F6 menu. Move the cursor to the parallelogram. When you see "THIS POLYGON," press ENTER. The calculator automatically displays the area of the parallelogram.

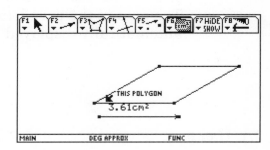

Try These

1. Select 1:Pointer on the F1 menu. Move the cursor to the point at the tip of the arrowhead of the vector. When you see "THIS POINT," hold down the Hand key and press the cursor pad to make the vector longer. Describe what happens to the parallelogram and the area.

2. Change the vector by dragging the point at the tip of the arrowhead to be to the left of the tail end of the vector. Do this slowly so that you can observe how the parallelogram and its area change. Describe what you observe.

1-6 The Geometer's Sketchpad

Area of Parallelograms

Use *The Geometer's Sketchpad* and the following steps to draw a parallelogram and find its area.

Step 1   Use the Segment tool to draw a segment that is neither horizontal nor vertical.

Step 2   Choose the Selection Arrow tool from the Toolbox and draw a selection marquee around the segment from Step 1.

Step 3   From the Edit menu, select Copy. Next, from the Edit menu select Paste. A copy of the original segment will appear alongside that segment. Drag the copy straight to the right to be a little farther from the original segment.

Step 4   Use the Segment tool to join the top ends of the two segments. Then join the bottom ends to complete the parallelogram.

Step 5   Now choose the Selection Arrow tool. Hold down the Shift key and select all four corners of the parallelogram. Go to the Construct menu and select Polygon Interior.

Step 6   Once the interior of the parallelogram is displayed as a shaded region, select it. Go to the Measure menu and choose Area. The area of the parallelogram is automatically displayed.

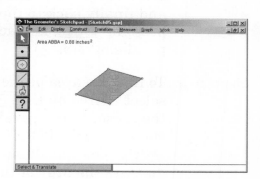

Try These

1. Drag the copy of the original segment to be still farther to the right of the original segment. Describe what happens to the area of the parallelogram as you do this.

2. Drag the copy of the segment back to the left. Do this so that the bottom point of the copy passes through or almost through the bottom point of the original. Describe how the parallelogram and its area change.

Midpoints in the Coordinate Plane

The Geometer's Sketchpad makes it easy for you to study segments and their midpoints in the coordinate plane. To display a coordinate, go to the Graph menu and select Create Axes. The computer will display a coordinate plane on which you can draw geometric figures.

Try These

1. Use the Segment tool to draw a segment in Quadrant I. With the segment selected, go to the Construct menu and choose Midpoint. Use the Text tool (the pointing finger) to label the endpoints and midpoint of the segment. Next use the Selection Arrow tool. Hold down the Shift key and select the endpoints and midpoint. Go to the Measure menu and choose Coordinates. The computer will display the coordinates of all three points. What do you notice about the coordinates of the midpoints?

2. Drag one endpoint of the segment into Quadrant III. How do the coordinates of the midpoint change as you do this?

3. Select the midpoint and one endpoint of the segment. On the Measure menu, choose Distance. The computer will display the distance between the two points. Use the same procedure to display the distance between the midpoint and the other endpoint. How are the two distances related? What happens if you drag an endpoint of the segment?

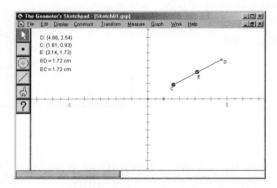

5

2-3

TI-92 Graphing Calculator

Separating a Segment into Segments of Almost Equal Length

You can separate a segment into two congruent parts by constructing its midpoint. What if you want to separate the segment into three or more congruent segments? Later in the text you will learn methods that can help you do this exactly. But you already know enough to use a TI-92 graphing calculator to get three or more almost congruent segments.

Step 1 Draw the segment that you would like to separate into congruent segments. Label the endpoints A and B.

Step 2 Below $\overline{AB}$, draw a horizontal segment CD. Go to the [F4] menu and choose 3:Midpoint. Move the cursor to point C. When the calculator displays "MIDPOINT BETWEEN THIS POINT," press [ENTER]. Move the cursor to point D and when you see "AND THIS POINT," press [ENTER]. The midpoint will appear in the middle of the segment. Label it E.

Step 3 Repeat Step 2 to construct the midpoint F of $\overline{CE}$. Repeat Step 2 one more time to construct the midpoint G of $\overline{ED}$.

Step 4 Now choose 1:Pointer on menu [F1] and drag point C to be on top of point A. Do this as accurately as you can.

Step 5 Drag point D so that point G lands on top of point B. When you do this, points F and E appear to land on $\overline{AB}$ and to separate it into three congruent segments.

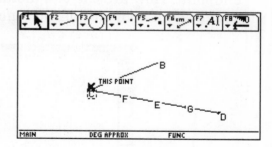

Try These

1. Do you think that this procedure could be used to separate a segment into more than three congruent segments? Explain.

2. Why is it necessary to say that points F and E only *appear* to separate $\overline{AB}$ into three congruent segments?

2-3 The Geometer's Sketchpad

Separating a Segment into Segments of Almost Equal Length

You can separate a segment into two congruent parts by constructing its midpoint. What if you want to separate the segment into three or more congruent segments? Later in the text you will learn methods that can help you do this exactly. But you already know enough to use *The Geometer's Sketchpad* to get three or more almost congruent segments.

Step 1   Draw the segment that you would like to separate into congruent segments. Label the endpoints A and B.

Step 2   Below $\overline{AB}$, draw a horizontal segment CD. Select $\overline{CD}$. Go to the Construct menu and choose Point at Midpoint. Label the midpoint that the computer displays as point E.

Step 3   Select points C and E. Go to the Construct menu and select Segment. Then choose Point at Midpoint from the Construct menu to display the midpoint of $\overline{CE}$. Label this midpoint F.

Step 4   Select points D and E. Go to the Construct menu and select Segment. Then choose Point at Midpoint from the Construct menu to display the midpoint of $\overline{DE}$. Label this midpoint G.

Step 5   Now use the Selection Arrow tool and drag point C to be on top of point A. Do this as accurately as you can.

Step 6   Drag point D so that point G lands on top of point B. When you do this, points F and E appear to land on $\overline{AB}$ and to separate it into three congruent segments.

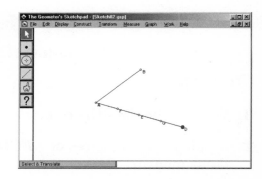

Try These

1. Do you think that this procedure could be used to separate a segment into more than three congruent segments? Explain.

2. Why is it necessary to say that points F and E only *appear* to separate segment AB into three congruent segments?

3-4

The Geometer's Sketchpad

Angle Bisectors for a Linear Pair

You can use *The Geometer's Sketchpad* to investigate how the angle bisectors for a linear pair are related.

Step 1   Use the Line tool to draw a line AB. Choose Point on Object on the Construct menu to construct a point C between A and B.

Step 2   Use the Ray tool to draw $\overrightarrow{CD}$.

Step 3   Use the Selection Arrow and select points D, C, and B, in that order. On the Construct menu, choose Angle Bisector to display the bisector of $\angle DCB$. With the angle bisector selected, choose Point on Object from the Construct menu to construct point E on the bisector of $\angle DCB$.

Step 4   Use the procedure from Step 3 to construct the bisector of $\angle DCA$. Construct point F on the bisector.

Step 5   Display the measure of $\angle FCE$. To do this, select points F, C, and E, in that order. Then go to the Measure menu and choose Angle.

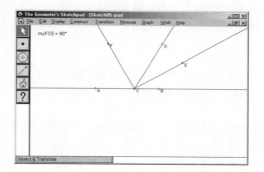

Try These

1. What value does the computer display for the measure of $\angle FCE$?

2. Display the measures of $\angle FCD$ and $\angle DCE$. What is the sum of these measures?

3. Drag point D. Describe what happens to the angle measures.

4. **Make a conjecture** about the relationship between bisectors of a linear pair.

3-6 TI-92 Graphing Calculator

Vertical Angles and Linear Pairs

You can use a TI-92 graphing calculator to investigate vertical angles and linear pairs.

Step 1 Draw a pair of lines that intersect. Choose 3:Intersection Point on the F2 menu. Move the cursor to one of the lines, and when you see "THIS LINE" displayed, press ENTER. Do the same for the other line. As soon as you press ENTER for the second line, the calculator displays the point where the two lines intersect. Label the point of intersection E, and label the other two points A and C.

Step 2 Next, choose 2:Point on Object on F2. Mark a point on $\overleftrightarrow{EA}$ that is on the opposite side of E from point A. Label the point B.

Step 3 Then mark a point on line EC that is on the opposite side of E from point C. Label this point D. The screen shows a sample result of following these steps.

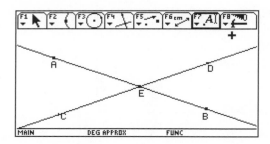

Try These

1. Make a list of all pairs of vertical angles in your figure. Use 3:Angle on the F6 menu to find the measures of the angles in each pair of vertical angles. What measures do you obtain? How are the measures of the vertical angles related?

2. Make a list of all the linear pairs of angles in your figure. Next, refer to the measures you found for the angles in Exercise 1. How are the measures of the angles in the linear pairs related?

3. Drag point C to a different location. Do the measures of the angles change? Do the relationships you described in Exercises 1 and 2 change?

3-6   The Geometer's Sketchpad

Vertical Angles and Linear Pairs

You can use *The Geometer's Sketchpad* to investigate vertical angles and linear pairs.

Step 1   Draw $\overleftrightarrow{AB}$. Next, draw $\overleftrightarrow{CD}$ so that it intersects $\overleftrightarrow{AB}$. Label the point of intersection E.

Step 2   To find the measures of the angles created by the intersecting lines, choose the Selection Arrow tool. Hold down the Shift key and click on each of the three points, A, E, and C, to select them. Choose Angle from the Measure menu to find the measure of the angle selected.

Step 3   Repeat this process to measure the other three angles. The screen shows a sample result of following these steps.

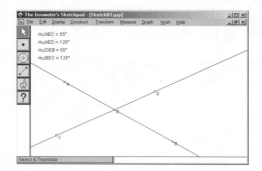

Try These

1. Make a list of all pairs of vertical angles in your figure. What measures do you obtain? How are the measures of the vertical angles related?

2. Make a list of all the linear pairs of angles in your figure. How are the measures of the angles in the linear pairs related?

3. Drag point C to a different location. Do the measures of the angles change? Do the relationships you described in Exercises 1 and 2 change?

4-5 The Geometer's Sketchpad

Slopes of Perpendicular Lines

You can use *The Geometer's Sketchpad* to study slopes of perpendicular lines.

Step 1 If necessary, clear the screen. To clear the screen for a new drawing, you can go to the Edit menu, choose Select All, and then choose Clear.

Step 2 Go to the Graph menu and choose Create Axes.

Step 3 Draw a pair of nonvertical perpendicular lines on the coordinate plane. One way to do this is to first use the Line tool to draw a nonvertical line. Next use the Point tool to draw a point not on the line. Select the line and the point. Then choose Perpendicular Line on the Construct menu.

Step 4 Use the pointing finger to label the perpendicular lines. Then select both lines. Choose Slope on the Measure menu to display the slopes of the lines.

Step 5 Use Calculate on the Measure menu to calculate the product of the slopes of the perpendicular lines.

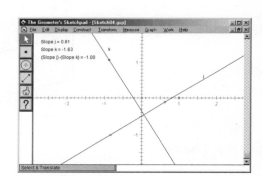

Try These

1. What number did you obtain as the product of the slopes of the perpendicular lines?

2. Select one of the points that you used to draw the first of your perpendicular lines. Drag this point to a different location. Describe what happens to the slopes of the perpendicular lines and to the product of the slopes.

3. Drag the point that you drew to construct the second of the perpendicular lines. Describe what happens to the lines and slopes when you do this.

4-3

TI-92 Graphing Calculator

Corresponding Angles and Parallel Lines

You can use a TI-92 calculator to investigate the measures of the angles formed by two parallel lines and a transversal.

Step 1   Use the Line tool on the F2 menu to draw a line. Use the Point tool on F2 to draw a second point on the line.

Step 2   Label the points on the line as A and B.

Step 3   Draw a line parallel to $\overleftrightarrow{AB}$. First use the Point tool on the F2 menu to draw a point C not on $\overleftrightarrow{AB}$. Then use the Parallel Line tool on the F4 menu to display the line through point C that is parallel to $\overleftrightarrow{AB}$. Draw a second point D on this line.

Step 4   Draw a line that intersects $\overleftrightarrow{AB}$ and $\overleftrightarrow{CD}$, as shown in the figure. Label points E and F on this line as shown. Mark and label the point G where $\overleftrightarrow{AB}$ and $\overleftrightarrow{EF}$ intersect. Mark and label the point H where $\overleftrightarrow{CD}$ and $\overleftrightarrow{EF}$ intersect.

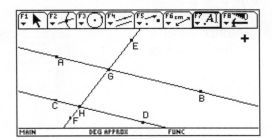

Try These

1. List the pairs of corresponding angles shown in your figure.

2. Use the Angle tool on the F6 menu to find the measures of the angles formed by the parallel lines and the transversal $\overleftrightarrow{EF}$. How do the measures of corresponding angles compare?

3. Drag one end of $\overleftrightarrow{EF}$ to a different position. Do the angle measures change? How do the measures of the corresponding angles compare?

4-3

The Geometer's Sketchpad

Corresponding Angles and Parallel Lines

You can use *The Geometer's Sketchpad* to investigate the measures of the angles formed by two parallel lines and a transversal.

Step 1 If you need to clear the screen, choose New Sketch from the File menu.

Step 2 Use the Line tool to draw a line. Label the two points shown on the line as A and B.

Step 3 Draw a line parallel to $\overleftrightarrow{AB}$. To do this, first use the Point tool to draw a point C not on $\overleftrightarrow{AB}$. Select the point and the line, and choose Parallel Line from the Construct menu. The computer displays the line parallel to $\overleftrightarrow{AB}$ through point C. Draw another point D on this new line.

Step 4 Use the Line tool to draw a line EF that intersects the two parallel lines, as shown in the figure.

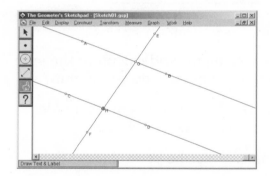

Try These

1. List the pairs of corresponding angles shown in your figure.

2. Use Angle on the Measure menu to find the measures of the angles formed by the parallel lines and the transversal $\overleftrightarrow{EF}$. How do the measures of corresponding angles compare?

3. Drag point F to a different location. Do the angle measures change? How do the measures of the corresponding angles compare?

5-2

The Geometer's Sketchpad

Angles of a Triangle

You can use *The Geometer's Sketchpad* to investigate the sum of the measures of the angles of a triangle.

Step 1   Use the Segment tool to draw triangle *ABC*. Label the triangle.

Step 2   Measure each angle of the triangle. Use Angle on the Measure menu.

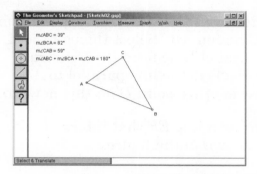

Try These

1. Choose Calculate on the Measure menu and calculate the sum of the angle measures from Step 2. What sum do you obtain?

2. Drag a vertex of the triangle. Do the measures of the angles change? Does the sum of the angle measures change?

3. Repeat Exercise 2 several times. Describe your observations.

4. **Make a conjecture** about the sum of the measures of the angles of any triangle.

5-4

TI-92 Graphing Calculator

Reflections and Congruent Triangles

You can use a TI-92 calculator to reflect a triangle over a line and compare the image to the original triangle.

Step 1   Use the Line tool on the ⎡F2⎤ menu to draw a line. On one side of the line, use the Triangle tool on the ⎡F3⎤ menu to draw a triangle.

Step 2   Choose the Reflection tool on the ⎡F5⎤ menu. Move the cursor to the triangle. When you see "REFLECT THIS TRIANGLE," press ⎡ENTER⎤. Then move the cursor to the line. When you see "WITH RESPECT TO THIS LINE," press ⎡ENTER⎤.

Step 3   Label the vertices of the triangles as shown in the figure.

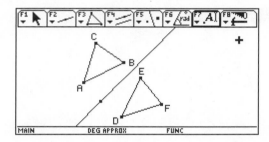

Try These

1. Use the Angle tool on the ⎡F6⎤ menu to measure the angles of each triangle. Then use the Distance & Length tool on the ⎡F6⎤ menu to find the lengths of the sides of the triangles. To find the length of a side, you will need to measure the distance between the endpoints of the side.
   a. How do the lengths of corresponding sides compare?
   b. How do the measures of corresponding angles compare?

2. Drag a vertex of $\triangle ABC$. How does doing this affect your answers for parts a and b of Exercise 1?

3. Make a conjecture about the relationship between a triangle and its reflection image over a line.

5-4

The Geometer's Sketchpad

Reflections and Congruent Triangles

You can use *The Geometer's Sketchpad* to reflect a triangle over a
line and compare the image to the original triangle.

Step 1   Use the Line tool to draw a line. On one side of the line,
use the Segment tool to draw a triangle.

Step 2   Select the line. Go to the Transform menu and choose
Mark Mirror. Select all the vertices and all the sides of
the triangle. Then choose Reflect on the Transform menu.
The computer will automatically display the reflection
image of the triangle across the line.

Step 3   Label the two points on the line and the vertices of the
triangles as shown in the figure.

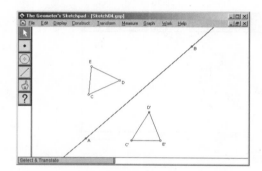

Try These

1. Use the Angle tool on the Measure menu to measure the angles
   of each triangle. Then use the Length tool on the Measure menu
   to find the lengths of the sides of the triangles.
   a. How do the measures of corresponding angles compare?
   b. How do the lengths of corresponding sides compare?

2. Drag a vertex of $\triangle ABC$. How does doing this affect your answers
   for parts a and b of Exercise 1?

3. Make a conjecture about the relationship between a triangle and
   its reflection image over a line.

Isosceles Triangles

You can use *The Geometer's Sketchpad* to draw an isosceles triangle
and study its properties.

Step 1   Draw a circle using the Circle tool. Label the center of
the circle point *A*. Label the point on the circle itself
point *B*.

Step 2   Use the point tool to draw a second point *C* on the circle.
Use the segment tool to draw △*ABC*.

Step 3   Select the circle. Go to the Display menu and choose Hide
Circle.

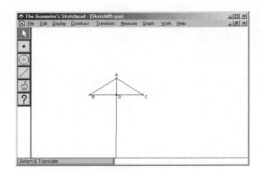

Try These

1. Tell how you can use the Measure menu to check that △*ABC* is
isosceles. Use your method to be sure it works.

2. Measure ∠*B* and ∠*C*. What is the relationship between ∠*B*
and ∠*C*?

3. Select ∠*BAC*. Be sure to select the points on the angle in the
correct order. Go to the Construct menu and choose Angle
Bisector. When the computer displays the bisector of ∠*BAC*, use
the Point tool to mark the point where the bisector intersects $\overline{BC}$.
Label the point of intersection *D*. What is point *D* in relation to
side $\overline{BC}$?

6-1

TI-92 Graphing Calculator

Medians and Centroids

You can use a TI-92 graphing calculator to study the medians of a triangle and to verify Theorem 6-1. You can draw and label the medians of a triangle and their point of intersection by using the following steps.

Step 1   Use the Triangle tool on the F2 menu to draw $\triangle ABC$.

Step 2   Choose the Midpoint tool on the F4 menu. Move the cursor to each side of the triangle. Each time you see "MIDPOINT OF THIS SIDE OF THE TRIANGLE," press ENTER.

Step 3   Use the Segment tool on the F2 menu to draw each median of the triangle. When you have done this, use the Intersection Point tool on the F2 menu to draw the point where the medians intersect.

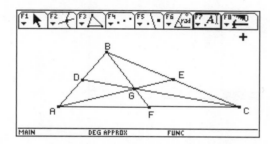

Try These

1. Measure the distance from A to G. Then measure the distance from G to E. How do the distances compare?

2. For each of the other medians, measure the distance from the vertex of the triangle to the centroid. Then measure the distance from the centroid to the midpoint. How do the distances compare?

3. Drag a vertex of $\triangle ABC$. Do your answers to Exercises 1 and 2 change or stay the same?

4. Draw a new triangle. Choose two vertices and draw the medians from those vertices. Then draw the line that passes through the third vertex and the point where the two medians intersect. Make a conjecture about the point where this line intersects the third side of the triangle. How can you use the calculator to check your conjecture? Try your idea to be sure it works.

6-1

The Geometer's Sketchpad

Medians and Centroids

You can use *The Geometer's Sketchpad* to study the medians of a triangle and to verify Theorem 6-1.

Step 1   Use the Segment tool to draw △*ABC*.

Step 2   Choose all three sides of the triangle. Then choose Point at Midpoint on the Construct menu.

Step 3   Use the Segment tool to draw each median of the triangle. When you have done this, select two of the medians. Choose Point at Intersection on the Construct menu. The computer will show the point where the medians intersect.

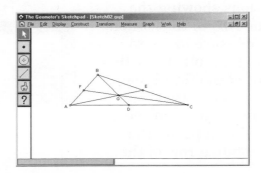

Try These

1. Measure the distance from *A* to *G*. Then measure the distance from *G* to *E*. How do the distances compare?

2. For each of the other medians, measure the distance from the vertex of the triangle to the centroid. Then measure the distance from the centroid to the midpoint. How do the distances compare?

3. Drag a vertex of △*ABC*. Do your answers to Exercises 1 and 2 change or stay the same?

4. Draw a new triangle. Choose two vertices and draw the medians from those vertices. Then draw the line that passes through the third vertex and the point where the two medians intersect. Make a conjecture about the point where this line intersects the third side of the triangle. How can you use the calculator to check your conjecture? Try your idea to be sure it works.

7-3

The Geometer's Sketchpad

Sides and Angles of Triangles

You can use *The Geometer's Sketchpad* to discover the special relationships between the side measures and angle measures of a triangle.

Step 1   Use the Segment tool to draw a triangle. Label the triangle *ABC*.

Step 2   Use Length and Angle on the Measure menu to display the measures of the sides and angles of △*ABC*.

Step 3   Select the equations showing the measures of ∠*BAC*, ∠*ABC*, and ∠*ACB*, in that order. Choose Tabulate from the Measure menu to display these measures in a table. Then select the equations showing the lengths of $\overline{BC}$, $\overline{CA}$, and $\overline{AB}$, in that order. Use Tabulate on the Measure menu to display these lengths in a table. Drag this table to be to the right of the first table, as shown in the figure. Notice that for each angle measure in the table on the left, the length of the side opposite the angle is in the corresponding row of the table on the right.

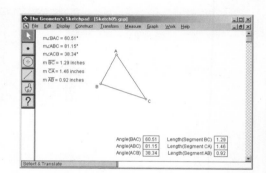

Try These

1. Refer to the triangle you drew using the steps above.
   a. What is the measure of the largest angle in your triangle?
   b. What is the measure of the side opposite the largest angle?
   c. What is the measure of the smallest angle in your triangle?
   d. What is the measure of the side opposite the smallest angle?

2. Drag vertex *A* to a different location.
   a. What are the lengths of the longest and shortest sides of the new triangle?
   b. What can you conclude about the measures of the angles of a triangle and the measures of the sides opposite these angles?

3. Select $\overline{AB}$ and choose Midpoint on the Construct menu. Select $\overline{AB}$ and its midpoint. Then choose Perpendicular Line on the Construct menu to display the perpendicular bisector of $\overline{AB}$. Drag vertex *C* very close to the perpendicular bisector. What do you observe about the measures of the sides and angles?

7-4

TI-92 Graphing Calculator

Verifying the Triangle Inequality Theorem

You can use a TI-92 graphing calculator to study the Triangle Inequality Theorem.

Step 1   Use the Circle tool on the [F3] menu to draw a circle with its center at point A. Use the Point on Object tool on the [F2] menu to mark a point P on the circle. Using P as the center, draw another circle. Use the Point on Object tool to mark a point Q on the second circle.

Step 2   Use the Triangle tool on the [F2] menu to draw $\triangle APQ$.

Step 3   Use the Hide/Show tool on the [F7] menu to hide the circles. Next, use the Distance & Length tool on the [F6] menu to measure $\overline{AP}$, $\overline{PQ}$, and $\overline{AQ}$. Use the Comment tool on the [F7] menu to display the measures as shown in the figure. Use the Calculate tool on the [F6] menu to display the sum of AP and PQ. Display the result (indicated by R:) as shown in the figure.

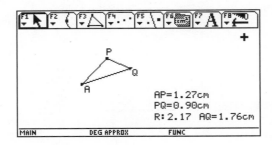

Try These

1. How does $AP + PQ$ compare with AQ?

2. Drag point Q to a different location. Describe what happens to the measures and to the relationship between $AP + PQ$ and AQ.

3. Try using the Animation tool on the [F7] menu to set point Q in motion. Watch the figure and the measurements. Describe your observations.

7-4

The Geometer's Sketchpad

Verifying the Triangle Inequality Theorem

You can use *The Geometer's Sketchpad* to study the Triangle Inequality Theorem.

Step 1   Use the Circle tool to draw a circle with its center at point A. Hide the point on the circle and use the Point tool to draw a different point C on the circle. Using C as center, draw another circle. Hide the point that is automatically shown on the circle. Use the Point tool to draw another point E on the second circle.

Step 2   Use the Segment tool to draw $\triangle ACE$.

Step 3   Hide the two circles. Then display the measures of the sides of $\triangle ACE$. Use Calculate on the Measure menu to display the sum of the lengths of $\overline{AC}$ and $\overline{CE}$.

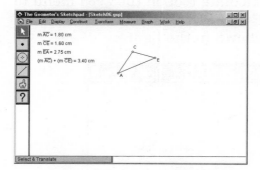

Try These

1. How does the sum of the lengths of $\overline{AC}$ and $\overline{CE}$ compare with the length of $\overline{EA}$?

2. Drag point E to a different location. Describe what happens to the measures and the relationship between the sum of the lengths of $\overline{AC}$ and $\overline{CE}$ and the length of $\overline{EA}$.

8-2

The Geometer's Sketchpad

Investigating Parallelograms

You can use *The Geometer's Sketchpad* to draw parallelograms and investigate their properties.

Step 1   Use the Segment tool to draw $\overline{AB}$ and $\overline{AC}$ that have a common endpoint A. Be sure the segments are not collinear. Label the endpoints.

Step 2   Select point B and $\overline{AC}$. Then choose Parallel Line on the Construct menu. The computer will display the line through B parallel to $\overline{AC}$. In a similar way, construct the line through point C parallel to $\overline{AB}$.

Step 3   Use the Point tool to mark the point D where the lines intersect. Label the point.

Step 4   Finally, use the Segment tool to draw $\overline{CD}$ and $\overline{BD}$. You now have a parallelogram whose properties can be studied using the Sketchpad.

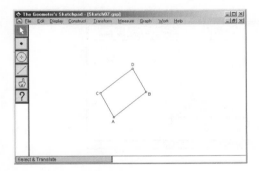

Try These

1. Use Angle on the Measure menu to verify that the opposite angles of a parallelogram are congruent. Describe your procedure.

2. Use Length on the Measure menu to verify that the opposite sides of a parallelogram are congruent. Describe your procedure.

3. Compare the measures of the angles in each pair of consecutive angles. Make a conjecture as to the relationship between consecutive angles in a parallelogram.

4. Draw the diagonals of $\square ABDC$. Mark and label the point E where the diagonals intersect. Measure $\overline{AE}$, $\overline{BE}$, $\overline{CE}$ and $\overline{DE}$. Make a conjecture about the diagonals of a parallelogram.

8-5

TI-92 Graphing Calculator

Isosceles Trapezoids

You can use a TI-92 graphing calculator to construct and study isosceles trapezoids.

Step 1   Use the Circle tool on the F3 menu to draw a circle with its center at point A. Use the Point on Object tool on the F2 menu to mark two points C and D on the circle and below point A. Use the Segment tool on the F2 menu to draw $\triangle ACD$.

Step 2   Use the Point on Object tool on the F2 menu to mark a point E between A and C on $\overline{AC}$. Use the Parallel Line tool on the F4 menu to draw the line through point E that is parallel to $\overline{CD}$. Use the Intersection Point tool on the F2 menu to mark the point G where this line intersects $\overline{AD}$. Use the Hide/Show tool on the F7 menu to hide point A, $\overline{AC}$ and $\overline{AD}$, and the circle. Finally, use the Segment tool on the F2 menu to draw $\overline{CE}$, $\overline{EG}$, and $\overline{GD}$. You now have a trapezoid.

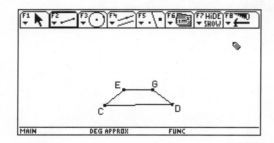

Try These

1. Use the tools on the F6 menu to verify that trapezoid $CEGD$ is isosceles. Describe the procedure for doing this.

2. Use the tools on the F6 menu to verify that the pairs of base angles are congruent. Describe the procedure for doing this.

3. Use the calculator to construct the midpoints of the sides of trapezoid $CEGD$. Join the midpoints to form a quadrilateral. Measure the sides of this quadrilateral. What kind of quadrilateral is it? How do you know?

8-5

The Geometer's Sketchpad

Isosceles Trapezoids

You can use *The Geometer's Sketchpad* to construct and study isosceles trapezoids.

Step 1 Use the Circle tool to draw a circle with center at point
A. Hide the point on the circle itself. Use the Point tool to
draw two new points *C* and *D* on the circle and below
point *A*. Use the Segment tool to draw △*ACD*.

Step 2 Use the Point tool to mark a point *E* between *A* and *C* on
$\overline{CD}$. Select point *E* and $\overline{CD}$. Then choose Parallel Line on
the Construct menu to have the computer display the
line through point *E* parallel to $\overline{CD}$. Use the Point tool to
mark the point *G* where this line intersects $\overline{AD}$. Next,
hide point *A*, $\overline{AC}$ and $\overline{AD}$, and the circle. Use the
Segment tool to draw $\overline{CE}$, $\overline{EG}$ and $\overline{GD}$. You now have a
trapezoid.

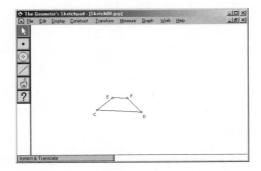

Try These

1. Use the tools on the Measure menu to verify that trapezoid
   CEGD is isosceles. Describe the procedure for doing this.

2. Use the tools on the Measure menu to verify that the pairs of
   base angles are congruent. Describe the procedure for doing this.

3. Use the Sketchpad to construct the midpoints of the sides of
   trapezoid *CEGD*. Join the midpoints to form a quadrilateral.
   Measure the sides of this quadrilateral. What kind of
   quadrilateral is it? How do you know?

The Geometer's Sketchpad

Ratios of Segments in Triangles

You can use *The Geometer's Sketchpad* to study the segments formed by a line parallel to one side of a triangle.

Step 1   Use the Segment tool to draw $\triangle ABC$.

Step 2   Use the Point tool to draw a point D between A and B. Label the point.

Step 3   Select point D and side $\overline{BC}$. Choose Parallel Line on the Construct menu to draw the line through D parallel to $\overline{BC}$.

Step 4   Use the Point tool to mark the point where the line intersects side $\overline{AC}$. Label the point E. You now have a figure that you can use to verify Theorem 9-5.

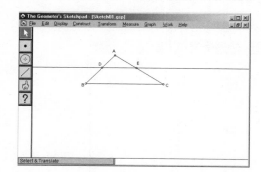

Try These

1. Use Distance on the Measure menu to find the lengths of $\overline{AD}$, $\overline{DB}$, $\overline{AE}$, and $\overline{EC}$.

2. Use Calculate on the Measure menu to calculate the value of $AD \div BD$ and $AE \div EC$. What can you say about these values?

3. Describe what happens to the segment lengths from Exercise 1 and the ratios from Exercise 2 when you drag D closer to A.

9-6 TI-92 Graphing Calculator

NAME _____ DATE _____ PERIOD _____

Expanding and Reducing Polygons

You can use a TI-92 graphing calculator to draw similar polygons and change their sizes. The procedure is illustrated below by using triangles, but the procedure works for polygons with more than three sides.

Step 1   Use the Segment tool on F2 to draw $\triangle ABC$. Label the vertices.

Step 2   Use the Point tool to draw a point D inside $\triangle ABC$. Use the Ray tool on F2 to draw rays from point D through each of the points A, B, and C.

Step 3   Use the Point tool to draw a point E outside $\triangle ABC$ and on $\overrightarrow{DA}$. Use the Parallel Line tool on F4 to draw the line through E parallel to $\overline{CA}$.

Step 4   Use the Point tool to mark the intersection point of the line and $\overrightarrow{DC}$. Use the Parallel Line tool to construct the line through F parallel to BC. Mark the point G where this line intersects $\overrightarrow{DB}$.

Step 5   Hide the lines but not the rays. Use the Segment tool on F2 to draw $\triangle EFG$. Your final figure should be similar to the one shown.

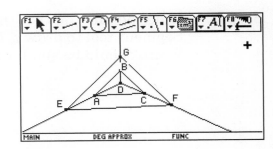

Try These

1. Is $\triangle EFG$ similar to $\triangle ACB$? Tell how you can use the TI-92 to find evidence to support your answer.

2. Drag point E farther away from point D. What happens to $\triangle EFG$? What happens to the ratios of the lengths of corresponding sides and to the angle measures?

3. Drag point E inside $\triangle ABC$. Describe what happens to $\triangle EFG$, the ratios, and the angle measures.

4. Try dragging other points in the figure. Describe what happens when you do this.

9-6

The Geometer's Sketchpad

Expanding and Reducing Polygons

You can use *The Geometer's Sketchpad* to draw similar polygons and change their sizes. The procedure is illustrated below by using triangles, but the procedure works for polygons with more than three sides.

Step 1   Use the Segment tool to draw $\triangle ABC$. Label the vertices.

Step 2   Use the Point tool to draw a point D inside $\triangle ABC$. Use the Ray tool to draw rays from point D through each of the points A, B, and C.

Step 3   Use the Point tool to draw a point E outside $\triangle ABC$ and on $\overrightarrow{DA}$. Select point E and $\overline{CA}$. Use Parallel Line on the Construct menu to draw the line through E parallel to $\overline{CA}$.

Step 4   Use the Point tool to mark the intersection point F of the line and $\overrightarrow{DC}$. Select F and $\overline{BC}$. Construct the line through F parallel to $\overline{BC}$. Mark the point G where this line intersects $\overrightarrow{DB}$.

Step 5   Hide the lines but not the rays. Use the Segment tool to draw $\triangle EFG$. Your final figure should be similar to the one shown.

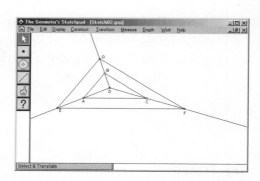

Try These

1. Is $\triangle EFG$ similar to $\triangle ACB$? Tell how you can use *The Geometer's Sketchpad* to find evidence to support your answer.

2. Drag point E farther away from point D. What happens to $\triangle EFG$? What happens to the ratios of the lengths of corresponding sides and to the angle measures?

3. Drag point E inside $\triangle ABC$. Describe what happens to $\triangle EFG$, the ratios, and the angle measures.

4. Try dragging other points in the figure. Describe what happens when you do this.

10-5

The Geometer's Sketchpad

Finding the Area of a Regular Polygon

You can use *The Geometer's Sketchpad* to study areas of regular polygons. Use the following steps to draw a regular hexagon.

Step 1   Use the Circle tool to draw a circle in the center of the screen. Use the Line tool to draw a horizontal line through the center of the circle.

Step 2   Mark the points where the line and circle intersect. Use the left-hand intersection point as center and draw a circle that passes through the center of the first circle. Do the same using the right-hand intersection point as the center of a third circle. Mark the points where the two new circles intersect the first circle. Label all the points. Your figure should look like the first figure shown below.

Step 3   Hide the line and the circles. Use the Segment tool to draw a hexagon that has point *A* as its center. You now have a regular hexagon, as shown in the second figure.

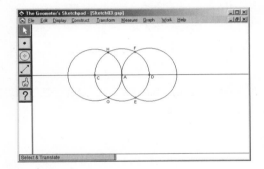 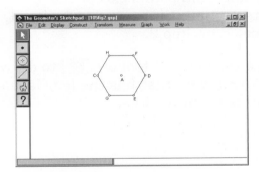

Try These

1. Select the bottom side of the hexagon and use Length on the Measure menu to display its length. Then select the center of the hexagon and the bottom side of the hexagon. Use Distance on the Measure menu to display the distance from the point to the segment. This distance is the length of an apothem.

2. Choose Calculate on the Measure menu to calculate the perimeter of the hexagon. Describe your procedure.

3. Use your result from Exercise 2, the distance from the center to the bottom side, and the formula for the area of a regular polygon to calculate the area of the hexagon.

4. Select the vertices of the hexagon. Choose Polygon Interior on the Construct menu. With the interior of the hexagon selected, choose Area on the Measure menu. Does the area that the computer displays agree with your result from Exercise 3?

10-4 TI-92 Graphing Calculator

Areas of Trapezoids

You can use a TI-92 graphing calculator to draw a trapezoid and study its area.

Step 1 Use the Line tool on [F2] to draw a horizontal line. Use the Point tool on [F2] to draw a point not on the line. Choose Parallel Line on [F4] and draw the line through this point parallel to the line.

Step 2 Draw two nonparallel lines that intersect the parallel lines. Use the Intersection Point tool on [F2] to mark the four points where these lines intersect the parallel lines. Label the points of intersection A, B, C, and D, as shown in the figure.

Step 3 Use the Hide/Show tool on [F7] to hide all lines and points except the intersection points you marked and labeled in Step 2.

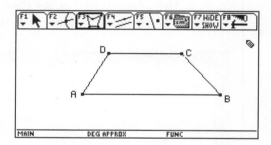

Step 4 Use the Polygon tool on [F3] to draw the trapezoid that has the four labeled points as its vertices.

Try These

1. Use the Distance & Length tool on [F6] to measure the distance from A to B. Then measure the distance from C to D. The resulting measures are the bases of the trapezoid.

2. Use the Hide/Show tool on [F7] to redisplay the line that contains the bottom side of the trapezoid. Use the Distance & Length tool on [F6] to find the distance from point C to this line. Once you have done this, hide the line again.

3. Use the results from Exercises 1 and 2 and the formula for the area of a trapezoid to calculate the area of the figure. Do this by using the Calculate tool on [F6].

4. Use the Area tool on [F6] to display the area of the trapezoid. Does the resulting area agree with the result you obtained in Exercise 3?

NAME _____ DATE _____ PERIOD _____

The Geometer's Sketchpad

Areas of Trapezoids

You can use *The Geometer's Sketchpad* to draw a trapezoid and study its area.

Step 1   Use the Line tool to draw a horizontal line. Use the Point tool to draw a point not on the line. Select this point and the line. Choose Parallel Line on the Construct menu to display the line through this point parallel to the line.

Step 2   Draw two nonparallel lines that intersect the parallel lines. Mark the four points where these lines intersect the parallel lines. Label the points of intersection.

Step 3   Select the lines and all the points except the intersection points you marked and labeled in Step 2. Choose Hide Objects on the Display menu.

Step 4   Use the Segment tool to draw the trapezoid that has the four labeled points as its vertices.

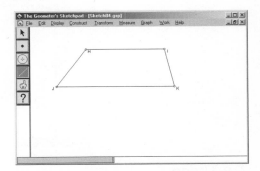

Try These

1. Measure the lengths of the parallel sides of the trapezoid.

2. Select the bottom side of the trapezoid and one of the top vertices. Choose Distance on the Measure menu. The distance the computer displays is equal to the height of the trapezoid.

3. Use the results from Exercises 1 and 2 and the formula for the area of a trapezoid to calculate the area of the figure. Do this by using Calculate on the Measure menu.

4. Select the vertices of the trapezoid. Choose Polygon Interior on the Construct menu. Select the interior of the trapezoid once it is displayed. Then choose Area on the Measure menu. Does this area agree with your result from Exercise 3?

NAME _____ DATE _____ PERIOD _____

The Geometer's Sketchpad

Investigating Circumference

You can use *The Geometer's Sketchpad* to find a relationship between the circumference and the diameter of a circle.

Step 1   Use the Circle tool to draw a circle. Label the center *A* and a point on the circle *B*.

Step 2   Use the Line tool to draw a line through the center of the circle.

Step 3   Use the Segment tool to draw the segment connecting the two points at which the line intersects the circle.

Step 4   Select the line. Then choose Hide Line on the Display menu.

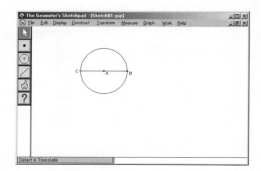

Try These

1. Select segment *BC*. Choose Length on the Measure menu to find the diameter of the circle. Next, select the circle and choose circumference on the Measure menu to display the circumference of the circle.

2. Use Calculate on the Measure menu to find the ratio of the circumference to the diameter.

3. Drag point *B* to make your circle larger. What happens to the diameter, the circumference, and the ratio of the circumference to the diameter?

32   *Geometry: Concepts and Applications*

11-4

TI-92 Graphing Calculator

Regular Octagons

You can use the Regular Polygon tool on a TI-92 graphing calculator to construct a regular octagon. However, there are other ways to construct regular polygons. The following steps can be used to draw a regular octagon.

Step 1   Use the Circle tool to draw a circle.

Step 2   Use the Line tool on `F2` to draw a line through the center of the circle.

Step 3   Use the Perpendicular Line tool on `F4` to draw the line through the center of the circle and perpendicular to the line from Step 2.

Step 4   Use the Angle Bisector tool on `F4` to bisect the angles of the figure in Step 3.

Step 5   Use the Segment tool to connect in order the points where the lines intersect the circle.

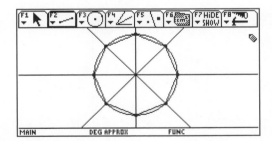

Try These

1. Measure the sides of the octagon you drew in Step 5. How are the lengths of the sides related?

2. Measure the angles of the octagon. How are the measures of the angles related?

3. Find a vertex that you can drag to make the octagon larger. When you make the octagon larger, the side lengths increase. Do the angle measures also increase?

11-4

The Geometer's Sketchpad

Regular Octagons

You can use *The Geometer's Sketchpad* to construct a regular octagon.

Step 1   Use the Circle tool to draw a circle.

Step 2   Use the Line tool to draw the line through the center of the circle and the point the computer displayed on the circle in Step 1.

Step 3   Select the center of the circle and the line. Choose Perpendicular Line on the Construct menu to draw the line perpendicular to the line from Step 2 at the center of the circle.

Step 4   Use Angle Bisector on the Construct menu to bisect each of the angles of the figure in Step 3.

Step 5   Use the Segment tool to connect in order the points where the lines and rays intersect the circle.

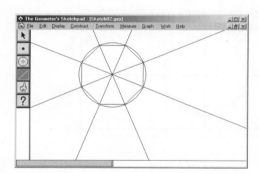

Try These

1. Measure the sides of the octagon you drew in Step 5. How are the lengths of the sides related?

2. Measure the angles of the octagon. How are the measures of the angles related?

3. Find a vertex that you can drag to make the octagon larger. When you make the octagon larger, the side lengths increase. Do the angle measures also increase?

12-2

The Geometer's Sketchpad

Drawing Nets for Prisms

You can use *The Geometer's Sketchpad* to draw a net for a triangular prism.

Try These

1. Draw an equilateral triangle a little to the left and above the middle of the screen. Adjust the position of the triangle to make its bottom side horizontal. Hide parts of your figure as needed to show only the equilateral triangle.

2. Draw a rectangle whose top is the bottom side of the triangle. Then construct an equilateral triangle that points downward and whose top is the bottom side of the rectangle. Hide parts of the figure as needed to leave only the triangles and rectangle. Describe your procedure.

3. Construct two rectangles to the right of the rectangle from Exercise 2 to obtain a figure like the one shown below. Describe your procedure.

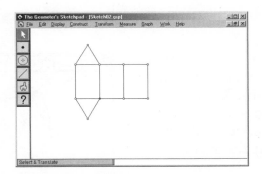

4. Use tools from the Measure menu to find the areas of the triangles and rectangles. If you cut out and folded this net to make a triangular prism, what would the lateral area and total surface area be?

12-4 TI-92 Graphing Calculator

Nets for Pyramids

You can use a TI-92 graphing calculator to draw nets for pyramids.

Try These

1. Use the TI-92 to draw an equilateral triangle.
   Describe how you can use reflections to obtain
   the figure shown at the right. Try your procedure
   to be sure it works. If you have access to a
   printer, you may want to print the figure, cut it
   out, and fold it to make the pyramid. You may
   want to enlarge the printout on a copier before
   making the pyramid.

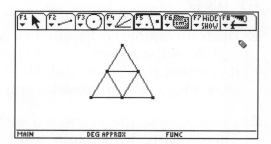

2. You can use a TI-92 to draw a net for a square
   pyramid. Begin by drawing a square that has its
   vertices on a circle, as shown in the figure at the
   right.

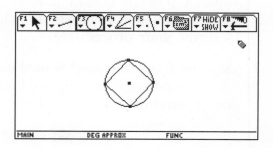

Next, draw a second circle whose radius is about
twice that of the first circle. Draw perpendicular
bisectors of the sides of the square. Mark the
points where these bisectors intersect the second
circle. Join these points to the vertices of the
square, as shown in the figure at the right.

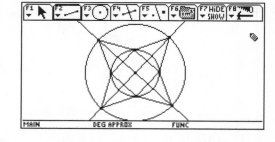

Finally, hide the circles and bisectors to display
the finished net. If you have access to a printer,
you may want to print the figure, cut it out, and
fold it to make the pyramid. You may want to
enlarge the printout on a copier before making
the pyramid.

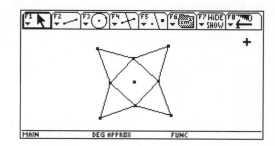

The Geometer's Sketchpad

Nets for Pyramids

You can use *The Geometer's Sketchpad* to draw nets for pyramids.

Try These

1. Use *The Geometer's Sketchpad* to draw an equilateral triangle. Describe how you can use reflections to obtain the figure shown at the right. Try your procedure to be sure it works. If you have access to a printer, you may want to print the figure, cut it out, and fold it to make the pyramid.

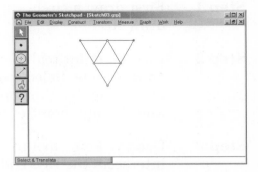

2. You can use *The Geometer's Sketchpad* to draw a net for a square pyramid. Begin by drawing a square that has its vertices on a circle, as shown in the figure at the right.

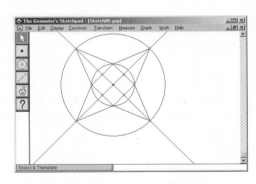

Next, draw a second circle whose radius is about twice that of the first circle. Draw perpendicular bisectors of the sides of the square. Mark the points where these bisectors intersect the second circle. Join these points to the vertices of the square, as shown in the figure at the right.

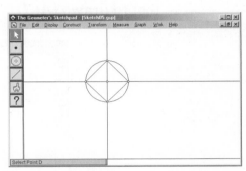

Finally, hide the circles and bisectors to display the finished net. If you have access to a printer, you may want to print the figure, cut it out, and fold it to make the pyramid.

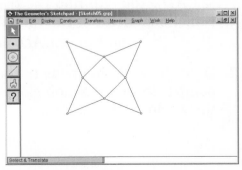

13-5

The Geometer's Sketchpad

A Trigonometric Identity

You can use *The Geometer's Sketchpad* to confirm that Theorem 13-3 states a trigonometric identity. Follow these steps to draw a figure like the one shown below.

Step 1   First draw a circle with center A. Use the Ray tool to draw $\overrightarrow{AB}$.

Step 2   Use the Point tool to mark a point C above the ray and on the circle. Select point C and the ray. Choose Perpendicular Line on the Construct menu to draw the line through point C perpendicular to the ray.

Step 3   Use the Point tool to mark the point D where the line intersects the ray. Hide the line. Then use the Segment tool to draw $\triangle ACD$.

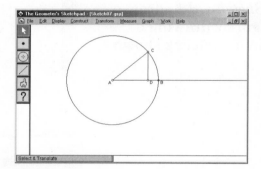

Try These

1. Measure $\angle CAD$. Drag point C to be close to point B, on the right side of the circle. Watch how the measure of $\angle CAD$ changes as you do this. Then drag point C to be close to the top of the circle. The possible measures of $\angle CAD$ are between what two numbers?

2. Use Calculate on the Measure menu to find $\frac{\sin{(\angle CAD)}}{\cos{(\angle CAD)}}$ and tan $(\angle CAD)$. You will find the trigonometric functions on the Functions menu of the Calculate panel. How do the values of $\frac{\sin{(\angle CAD)}}{\cos{(\angle CAD)}}$ and tan $(\angle CAD)$ compare?

3. Describe what happens to the values in Exercise 2 as you drag point C from a position close to B to a position close to the top of the circle.

13-4

TI-92 Graphing Calculator

Finding Tangent Ratios

You can use a TI-92 graphing calculator to study trigonometric ratios such as the tangent ratio. Use the following steps to construct a right triangle.

Step 1   Use the Line tool on [F2] to draw a horizontal line through a point C. Use the Perpendicular Line tool on [F4] to draw the line perpendicular to the horizontal line at point C.

Step 2   Use the Point on Object tool on [F2] to draw a point B above C on the vertical line. Draw a point A to the left of point C on the horizontal line.

Step 3   Hide the two lines. Use the Segment tool on [F2] to draw $\triangle ABC$.

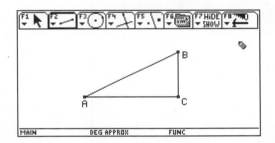

Try These

1. Use the <u>Distance & Length</u> tool on [F6] to find the lengths of $\overline{BC}$ and $\overline{AC}$. Use the Calculate tool on [F6] to find the ratio of BC to AC.

2. Use the Angle tool on [F6] to find the measure of $\angle A$. Then use the Calculate tool to find the tangent for the measure of $\angle A$. Use the [TAN] key on the TI-92. You may find it helpful to use the Comment tool on [F7] to display your work in an organized way.

3. How does the ratio from Exercise 1 compare with the value of the tangent from Exercise 2?

4. Drag point A to several different locations. What happens to the segment measures, their ratio, and the value of tan A as you do this?

13-4 The Geometer's Sketchpad

Finding Tangent Ratios

You can use *The Geometer's Sketchpad* to study trigonometric ratios such as the tangent ratio. Use the following steps to construct a right triangle.

Step 1   Draw a horizontal line AB. Select point A and the line. Choose Perpendicular Line on the Construct menu to draw the line perpendicular to $\overleftrightarrow{AB}$ at point A.

Step 2   Use the Point tool to draw a point C above point A on the vertical line. Draw a point D to the left of point A on the horizontal line.

Step 3   Hide point B and the two lines. Use the Segment tool to draw $\triangle ACD$.

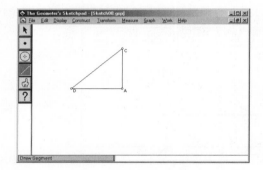

Try These

1. Use the Length tool on the Measure menu to find the lengths of CA and DA. Use Angle on the Measure menu to find the measure of $\angle CDA$.

2. Use Calculate on the Measure menu to calculate the ratio of CA to DA.

3. On the Calculate panel, click on Functions and choose tan(. Use the measure of $\angle CDA$ from Exercise 1 to display tan ($\angle CDA$). How does the result compare with the ratio you found in Exercise 2?

4. Drag point D to several different locations. What happens to the segment measures, their ratio, and the value of tan ($\angle CDA$) as you do this?

The Geometer's Sketchpad

Investigating Tangent-Tangent Angles

You can use *The Geometer's Sketchpad* to verify the relationship between a tangent-tangent angle and its intercepted arcs stated in Theorem 14-12.

The figure at the right shows an acute angle, $\angle Q$. To verify Theorem 14-12, you can measure $\angle Q$, find the measures of the intercepted arcs, and then perform the calculation.

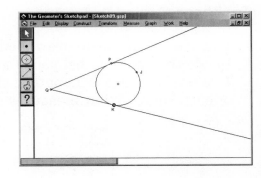

Try These

1. Use *The Geometer's Sketchpad* to construct and label a figure like the one shown. Then use Angle on the Measure menu to measure $\angle Q$. What measure do you get?

2. How can you use Angle on the Measure menu to find $m\widehat{PK}$ and $m\widehat{PJK}$? Use your method to find these measures. What are the results?

3. Use Calculate on the Measure menu to find $\frac{1}{2}(m\widehat{PJK} - m\widehat{PK})$. How does the result compare with $m\angle Q$ from Exercise 1? Is your answer in agreement with Theorem 14-12?

4. Drag point Q farther away from the center of the circle. Describe how this affects the arc measures and the measure of $\angle Q$.

5. Suppose you change $\angle Q$ to an obtuse angle. Do the results from Exercises 1-3 change? Explain your answer.

14-5

TI-92 Graphing Calculator

Circles and Segment Measures

You can use a TI-92 graphing calculator to verify theorems about circles and segment measures.

Try These

1. Use the calculator to draw a circle and two chords that intersect inside the circle. Label your figure as shown in the figure below. Use the Distance & Length tool on F6 to measure the segments of each chord. What measures do you get?

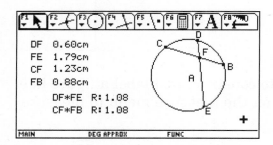

2. Use the Calculate tool on F6 to find the products $DF \cdot FE$ and $CF \cdot FB$. How are the products related?

3. Use the Comment tool on F7 to show your results in an organized way. Drag an endpoint of one of the chords. Do the measures of the segments of the chords change? Do the products change?

4. Draw and label a figure like the one shown for Theorem 14-14 on page 613 of the Student Edition. Use the TI-92 to verify the theorem.

5. Use the figure you drew for Exercise 4. Use the Calculate tool to find the value of $(JD)^2$. Drag a point in the figure to place point L as close to point D as you can. When you do this, how does $JK \cdot JC$ compare with $(JD)^2$?

NAME _____ DATE _____ PERIOD _____

The Geometer's Sketchpad

Circles and Segment Measures

You can use *The Geometer's Sketchpad* to verify theorems about circles and segment measures.

Try These

1. Use *The Geometer's Sketchpad* to draw a circle and two chords that intersect inside the circle. Label your figure as shown in the figure below. Use Length tool on the Measure menu to measure the segments of each chord. What measures do you get?

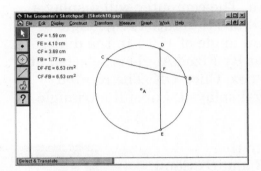

2. Use the Calculate tool on the Measure menu to find the products $DF \cdot FE$ and $CF \cdot FB$. How are the products related?

3. Drag an endpoint of one of the chords. Do the measures of the segments of the chords change? Do the products change?

4. Draw and label a figure like the one shown for Theorem 14-14 on page 613 of the Student Edition. Use *The Geometer's Sketchpad* to verify the theorem.

5. Use the figure you drew for Exercise 4. Use Calculate to find the value of $(JD)^2$. Drag a point in the figure to place point L as close to point D as you can. When you do this, how does $JK \cdot JC$ compare with $(JD)^2$?

16-5 The Geometer's Sketchpad

Rotating a Triangle

You can use *The Geometer's Sketchpad* to rotate figures about a selected point using a given angle.

Step 1   Draw a triangle by using the Segment tool. Label the triangle *ABC*.

Step 2   Draw the point *D* about which you want to rotate the triangle. Choose Mark Center on the Transform menu.

Step 3   Select all vertices and sides of △*ABC*. Choose Rotate from the transform menu. The computer will display a dialog box. Suppose you want to rotate the triangle counterclockwise using an angle of 120°. In the dialog box, type 120. Check that By Fixed Angle is selected at the bottom of the dialog box. Click OK. The rotated triangle is automatically displayed. Label the triangle *A'B'C'*.

Step 4   Draw segments from *D* to the corresponding vertices *B* and *B'*. Show these as dashed segments to make them stand out. (Go to Line Style on the Display menu to select this option.) Then draw segments from *D* to the corresponding vertices *C* and *C'*.

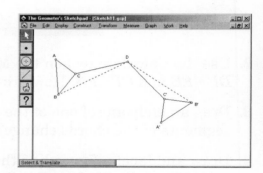

Try These

1. Use Angle on the Measure menu to measure ∠*BDB'* and ∠*CDC'*.

2. What is the relation of the angle measures from Exercise 1 to the angle measure you used for the rotation?

3. Describe what happens to the angle measures if you drag point *D* to a different location.

4. Delete △*A'B'C'*. Repeat Steps 3 and 4 using an angle measure of 110. What happens to the image of the original triangle? What measure do you get when you measure ∠*BDB'* and ∠*CDC'*?

16-4

TI-92 Graphing Calculator

Reflecting a Figure Over a Line

You can use a TI-92 graphing calculator to study reflections of figures in the coordinate plane.

Try These

1. Display a coordinate plane on the screen. Recall that you can do this by choosing Format on F8 . Highlight Coordinate Axes, then highlight Rectangular. Press ENTER twice. After the coordinate axes are displayed, use the Triangle tool on F3 to draw a triangle. Label the triangle *ABC*. Use the Reflection tool on F5 to reflect $\triangle ABC$ over the *y*-axis. Label the corresponding vertices for *A*, *B*, and *C* as *X*, *Y*, and *Z*.

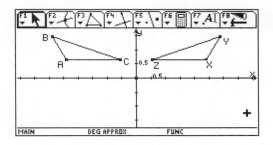

2. Use Equation & Coordinates on F6 to display the coordinates of corresponding vertices *A* and *X*. How are the coordinates of these points related?

3. Repeat Exercise 2 for the other corresponding vertices of $\triangle ABC$ and $\triangle XYZ$. Does the relationship you described for Exercise 2 still hold true?

4. Reflect $\triangle ABC$ over the *x*-axis. How are the coordinates of corresponding vertices related?

5. Clear the drawings from the screen and use the Triangle tool to draw a new triangle on the coordinate plane. Use the Angle Bisector tool on F4 to bisect the angle formed by the positive part of the *x*-axis and the positive part of the *y*-axis. Reflect your new triangle over this angle bisector. How are the coordinates of corresponding vertices related?

16-4 The Geometer's Sketchpad

Reflecting a Figure Over a Line

You can use *The Geometer's Sketchpad* to study reflections of figures in the coordinate plane.

Try These

1. Display a coordinate plane on the screen. Recall that you can do this by choosing Create Axes from the Graph menu. Use the segment tool to draw a triangle. Label the triangle *CDE*. Select the *y*-axis and choose Mark Mirror from the Transform menu. Select all the vertices and sides of △*CDE*. Then choose Reflect from the Transform menu. Label the vertices of the image triangle *C'D'E'*.

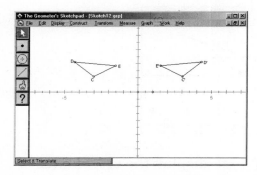

2. Use Coordinates on the Measure menu to display the coordinates of corresponding vertices *C* and *C'*. How are the coordinates of these points related?

3. Repeat Exercise 2 for the other corresponding vertices of △*CDE* and △*C'D'E'*. Does the relationship you described for Exercise 2 still hold true?

4. Reflect △*CDE* over the *x*-axis. How are the coordinates of corresponding vertices related?

5. Clear the drawings from the screen and use the Segment tool to draw a new triangle on the coordinate plane. Use Angle Bisector on the Construct menu to bisect the angle formed by the positive part of the *x*-axis and the positive part of the *y*-axis. Reflect your new triangle over this angle bisector. How are the coordinates of corresponding vertices related?

Answers

Page 2, Lesson 1-5

1. The new figure is inside the second figure. It looks like the original figure, only it is smaller. **2.** There are six 4-sided figures. The first, third, and fifth look alike, but are different sizes. The second, fourth, and sixth figures look alike, but are different sizes.

Page 3, Lesson 1-6

1. The parallelogram gets longer across the bottom and the area increases.
2. The parallelogram gets shorter across the bottom and the area decreases. The area appears to decrease all the way to 0 and then to increase again as you move the tip of the vector farther to the left.

Page 4, Lesson 1-6

1. The parallelogram gets longer across the bottom and the area increases.
2. The parallelogram gets shorter across the bottom and the area decreases. If the copy is dragged to be to the left of the original segment, the area appears to decrease all the way to 0 and then to increase again as you move farther to the left of the original segment.

Page 5, Lesson 2-5

1. They are both positive. **2.** They decrease. **3.** They are equal; both distances change, but they remain equal to each other.

Page 6, Lesson 2-3

1. Sample answer: Yes; you can use more midpoints for the segments on $\overline{CD}$. By choosing just the right point to land on point B when you drag point D, you can get more segments of equal length on $\overline{AB}$. **2.** When you drag point C to put it on top of point A, it may not be exactly on top of point A, but only very close. When you drag point D, point G might not land exactly on point B, but only very close.

Page 7, Lesson 2-3

1. Sample answer: Yes; you can use more midpoints for the segments on $\overline{CD}$. By choosing just the right point to land on point B when you drag point D, you can get more segments of equal length on $\overline{AB}$. **2.** When you drag point C to put it on top of point A, it may not be exactly on top of point A, but only very close. When you drag point D, point G might not land exactly on point B, but only very close.

Page 8, Lesson 3-4

1. 90 **2.** 90 **3.** The measure of $\angle FCE$ does not change. The measures of $\angle FCD$ and $\angle DCE$ change, but their sum continues to be 90. **4.** The bisectors of the angles of a linear pair are perpendicular.

Page 9, Lesson 3-6

1. $\angle AEC$ and $\angle BED$; $\angle BEC$ and $\angle AED$; angle measures will vary; the vertical angles have equal measures.
2. $\angle AEC$ and $\angle AED$; $\angle AED$ and $\angle DEB$; $\angle DEB$ and $\angle BEC$; $\angle BEC$ and $\angle AEC$; the measures for each linear pair have a sum of 180. **3.** yes; no

Page 10, Lesson 3-6

1. $\angle AEC$ and $\angle BED$; $\angle BEC$ and $\angle AED$; angle measures will vary; the vertical angles have equal measures.
2. $\angle AEC$ and $\angle AED$; $\angle AED$ and $\angle DEB$; $\angle DEB$ and $\angle BEC$; $\angle BEC$ and $\angle AEC$; the measures for each linear pair have a sum of 180. **3.** yes; no

Page 11, Lesson 3-6

1. ∠*AEC* and ∠*BED*; ∠*BEC* and ∠*AED*; angle measures will vary; the vertical angles have equal measures. **2.** ∠*AEC* and ∠*AED*; ∠*AED* and ∠*DEB*; ∠*DEB* and ∠*BEC*; ∠*BEC* and ∠*AEC*; the measures for each linear pair have a sum of 180. **3.** yes; no

Page 11, Lesson 4-5

1. −1.000 **2.** The slopes change, but their product remains equal to −1. **3.** The second line appears to move parallel to its original position. The slopes and their product do not change.

Page 12, Lesson 4-3

1. ∠*AGE* and ∠*CHG*, ∠*AGH* and ∠*CHF*, ∠*EGB* and ∠*GHD*, ∠*BGH* and ∠*DHF* **2.** They are equal. **3.** Yes; they remain equal.

Page 13, Lesson 4-3

1. ∠*AGE* and ∠*CHG*, ∠*AGH* and ∠*CHF*, ∠*EGB* and ∠*GHD*, ∠*BGH* and ∠*DHF* **2.** They are equal. **3.** Yes; they remain equal.

Page 14, Lesson 5-2

1. 180 **2.** yes; no **3.** The angle measures change each time, but the sum of the angle measures continues to be 180. **4.** The sum of the measures of the angles of any triangle is 180.

Page 15, Lesson 5-4

1a. They are equal. **1b.** They are equal. **2.** The answers remain the same, even though the lengths of the sides and the measures of the angles changed. **3.** If you reflect a triangle over a line, the image triangle is congruent to the original triangle.

Page 16, Lesson 5-4

1a. They are equal. **1b.** They are equal. **2.** The answers remain the same, even though the lengths of the sides and the measures of the angles changed. **3.** If you reflect a triangle over a line, the image triangle is congruent to the original triangle.

Page 17, Lesson 6-4

1. Sample answer: Select $\overline{AB}$ and choose Length on the Measure menu to display the length of the segment. In the same way, display the length of $\overline{AC}$. The lengths are equal, and this shows that △*ABC* is isosceles. **2.** They are congruent. **3.** It appears to be the midpoint of $\overline{BC}$.

Page 18, Lesson 6-1

1. The distance from *A* to *G* is twice the distance from *G* to *E*. **2.** In each case, the distance from the vertex to the centroid is twice the distance from the centroid to the midpoint. **3.** They are the same. **4.** Sample answer: The point where the line intersects the third side is the midpoint of the third side. To check this, measure the distance from this point to each endpoint of the third side. The distances are equal.

Page 19, Lesson 6-1

1. The distance from *A* to *G* is twice the distance from *G* to *E*. **2.** In each case, the distance from the vertex to the centroid is twice the distance from the centroid to the midpoint. **3.** They are the same. **4.** Sample answer: The point where the line intersects the third side is the midpoint of the third side. To check this, measure the distance from this point to each endpoint of the third side. The distances are equal.

Page 20, Lesson 7-3

1a–d. See students' work.   **2a.** See students' work.   **2b.** Sample answer: The largest angle of a triangle is opposite the longest side. The smallest angle of a triangle is opposite the shortest side.   **3.** Sample answer: The measures of the angles at A and B are almost equal, and the lengths of $\overline{CA}$ and $\overline{CB}$ are almost equal.

Page 21, Lesson 7-4

1. $AP + PQ$ is greater than AQ.
2. The measures of $\overline{AP}$ and $\overline{PQ}$ do not change, and neither does their sum. The measure of $\overline{AQ}$ does change, but it remains less than $AP + PQ$.   **3.** The same observations that were made in Exercise 2 apply here as well.

Page 22, Lesson 7-4

1. The sum is greater than the length of $\overline{EA}$.   **2.** The lengths of $\overline{AC}$ and $\overline{CE}$ do not change and neither does their sum. The length of $\overline{EA}$ does change, but it remains less than the sum of the lengths of $\overline{AC}$ and $\overline{CE}$.

Page 23, Lesson 8-2

1. See students' work.   **2.** See students' work.   **3.** Consecutive angles of a parallelogram are supplementary.
4. The diagonals of a parallelogram bisect each other.

Page 24, Lesson 8-5

1. Measure $\overline{CE}$ and $\overline{DG}$, which are the sides that are not parallel. Choose Distance & Length on the ⌐F6⌐ menu to display the lengths of the two sides. The lengths of these sides are equal, so the trapezoid is isosceles.   **2.** Use Angle on the ⌐F6⌐ menu to display the measures of $\angle ECD$ and $\angle GDC$. Do the same for $\angle CEG$ and $\angle DGE$. For each pair of

angles, the measures are equal. This means that the pairs of base angles are congruent.   **3.** Rhombus; opposite sides have equal measures, so the quadrilateral is a parallelogram. Since all the sides have equal measures, it is a rhombus.

Page 25, Lesson 8-5

1. Select sides $\overline{CE}$ and $\overline{DG}$, which are the sides that are not parallel. Choose Length on the Measure menu to display the lengths of the two sides. The lengths of these sides are equal, so the trapezoid is isosceles.   **2.** Use Angle on the Measure menu to display the measures of $\angle ECD$ and $\angle GDC$. Do the same for $\angle CEG$ and $\angle DGE$. For each pair of angles, the measures are equal. This means that the pairs of base angles are congruent.   **3.** Rhombus; opposite sides have equal measures, so the quadrilateral is a parallelogram. Since all the sides have equal measures, it is a rhombus.

Page 26, Lesson 9-4

1. See students' work.   **2.** The ratios are equal.   **3.** The lengths of $\overline{AD}$ and $\overline{AE}$ get smaller, and the lengths of $\overline{DB}$ and $\overline{EC}$ get larger. The ratios get smaller but remain equal to each other.

Page 27, Lesson 9-6

1. Sample answer: Measure the sides and angles of the triangles. Calculate $AB \div EG$, $BC \div GF$, and $CA \div FE$. When you do this, you find that all the ratios are equal. Measure the corresponding angles. Measures of corresponding angles are equal. Since their side lengths are proportional and corresponding angles are congruent, the triangles are similar.

2. △*EFG* gets bigger. All the ratios decrease, but they remain equal to each other. The angle measures do not change, so corresponding angles are still congruent.   **3.** △*EFG* shrinks and moves to the inside of △*ABC*. All the ratios increase but remain equal. Measures of angles do not change.
4. Answers will vary depending on which point is dragged. See students' work.

Page 28, Lesson 9-6

1. Sample answer: Measure the sides and angles of the triangles. Calculate *AB* ÷ *EG*, *BC* ÷ *GF*, and *CA* ÷ *FE*. When you do this, you find that all the ratios are equal. Measure the corresponding angles. Measures of corresponding angles are equal. Since their side lengths are proportional and corresponding angles are congruent, the triangles are similar.   **2.** △*EFG* gets bigger. All the ratios decrease, but they remain equal to each other. The angle measures do not change, so corresponding angles are still congruent.   **3.** △*EFG* shrinks and moves to the inside of △*ABC*. All the ratios increase but remain equal. Measures of angles do not change.
4. Answers will vary depending on which point is dragged. See students' work.

Page 29, Lesson 10-5

1. Lengths and distances will vary. See students' work.   **2.** Perimeters will vary. Sample answer: Multiply the length of the bottom side of the hexagon by 6.
3. Answers will vary. See students' work.   **4.** yes

Page 30, Lesson 10-4

1-3. See students' work.   **4.** yes

Page 31, Lesson 10-4

1-3. See students' work.   **4.** yes

Page 32, Lesson 11-5

1. See students' work.   **2.** 3.14   **3.** The diameter and circumference get larger. The ratio stays the same.

Page 33, Lesson 11-4

1. The lengths are all equal.   **2.** The angle measures are all equal to 135.
3. no

Page 34, Lesson 11-4

1. The lengths are all equal.   **2.** The angle measures are all equal to 135.
3. no

Page 35, Lesson 12-2

1-4. See students' work.

Page 36, Lesson 12-4

1-4. See students' work.

Page 37, Lesson 12-4

1-4. See students' work.

Page 38, Lesson 13-5

1. 0 and 90   **2.** They are equal.   **3.** The values increase, but the ratio of sine to cosine remains equal to the tangent.

Page 39, Lesson 13-4

1-2. See students' work.   **3.** The two values are equal.   **4.** As point *A* gets closer to *C*, the length of $\overline{AC}$ decreases. The length of $\overline{BC}$ stays the same. So the ratio of *BC* to *AC* increases, as does the value of tan *A*. As point *A* gets farther from *C*, *AC* increases, while *BC* stays the same. So the ratio of *BC* to *AC* decreases, as does the value of tan *A*.

Page 40, Lesson 13-4

1-2. See students' work.   3. It is equal to the ratio from Exercise 2.   4. If you drag D to be closer to point A, then CA stays the same, but DA decreases. The ratio of CA to DA increases, which means that the tangent of $\angle CDA$ increases. If you drag D to be farther away from A, then CA stays the same, but DA increases. The ratio of CA to DA decreases, which means that the tangent of $\angle CDA$ decreases.

Page 41, Lesson 14-4

1. Answers will vary.   2. Sample answer: Find the measure of the minor arc, $\overset{\frown}{PK}$, by measuring the corresponding central angle. Subtract the result from 360 to find the measure of the major arc, $\overset{\frown}{PJK}$; measures will vary.   3. The results are equal; yes.
4. The measure of $\overset{\frown}{PK}$ increases and the measure of $\overset{\frown}{PJK}$ decreases; the measure of $\angle Q$ decreases.   5. The results from Exercises 1 and 2 change. The measure of $\angle Q$ increases, the measure of $\overset{\frown}{PK}$ decreases, and the measure of $\overset{\frown}{PJK}$ increases. However, the result from Exercise 3 does not change. The value of $\frac{1}{2}(m\overset{\frown}{PJK} - m\overset{\frown}{PK})$ increases and equals the greater value of $m\angle Q$ after $\angle Q$ changes from an acute to an obtuse angle.

Page 42, Lesson 14-5

1. Answers will vary.   2. They are equal.   3. yes; no   4. See students' work.   5. See students' work. $JK \cdot JC$ and $(JD)^2$ will be equal or almost equal when L is moved very close to D.

Page 43, Lesson 14-5

1. Answers will vary.   2. They are equal.   3. yes; no   4. See students' work.   5. See students' work. $JK \cdot JC$ and $(JD)^2$ will be equal or almost equal when L is moved very close to D.

Page 44, Lesson 16-5

1. See students' work.   2. Both equal the angle measure of rotation.   3. They still equal 120.   4. The location of the image of $\triangle ABC$ changes. The measures of $\angle BDB'$ and $\angle CDC'$ are 110.

Page 45, Lesson 16-4

1. See students' work.   2. The x-coordinates are opposites. The y-coordinates are equal.   3. yes
4. The x-coordinates of corresponding vertices are equal. The y-coordinates are opposites.   5. The coordinates of corresponding vertices are the same numbers but in the opposite order.

Page 46, Lesson 16-4

1. See students' work.   2. The x-coordinates are opposites. The y-coordinates are equal.   3. yes
4. The x-coordinates of corresponding vertices are equal. The y-coordinates are opposites.   5. The coordinates of corresponding vertices are the same numbers but in the opposite order.